Acknowledgement

To little Veer – in the hope that he will battle through his Fanconi Anaemia and continue to be our hero for many years to come.

IN AID OF ANTHONY NOLAN

saving the lives
of people with
blood cancer

Anthony Nolan is a registered charity no. 803716 / SCO38827

Published by The Jai Jais 2020
Copyright Sunita Shah and James Ballance
All rights reserved
The Jai Jais is a Registered Trademark of The Jai Jais Limited
The moral right of the authors and illustrator has been asserted
ISBN 978-1-91623-420-6

Other titles are available in the Jai Jais Series.
Go online to discover more at www.thejaijais.com

The Jai Jais®

Mahavir

by Sunita Shah and Nirav Gudhka

Illustrated by James Ballance

Thousands of years ago there was a magnificent kingdom in India called Kundapur. It was ruled by King Siddhartha and Queen Trishla. They were respected and loved by all. There was peace and harmony across the land, because everyone in the kingdom was treated fairly.

One night, while Queen Trishla was sleeping in her chambers, she was dreaming. Vision after vision came into her mind: she saw a fearless lion, a splendid elephant, a golden shining sun, precious jewels and the beautiful goddess Lakshmi. More intriguing visions like these entered her dreams that night.

When she awoke and told King Siddhartha, he explained that the dreams were a sign that she was going to give birth to a brave and glorious son. He would spread wisdom far and wide and bring happiness to all around. The Queen was amazed to realise that she was to be the mother of a Tirthankar, one of the special gods of Jainism.

2.

Nine months later Queen Trishla did indeed give birth to a son. She and the King were overjoyed and named him Vardhaman.

The birth was celebrated with joy and excitement throughout the kingdom. Saudharma Indra, the ruler of the first of the sixteen heavens, descended from above, along with his wife Sacchi Indrani. They came to bless the new baby. Many other heavenly beings also came to join in the festivities.

Saudharma Indra took baby Vardhaman on a long journey to a gigantic mountain called Mount Meru. They rode on a magnificent elephant, called an Airavat. This ancient elephant had many trunks and tusks. They travelled all the way up the enormous mountain, and at the very top Saudharma Indra gave baby Vardhaman his very first bath.

4.

Vardhaman was not born a god. Through his life's journey and experiences, he developed into a god. The same is true for any of the previous gods, and those gods that will come in the future.

As a royal prince, Vardhaman lived a life of great wealth and luxury. The palace in Kundapur, located in modern-day Bihar, was a place of splendour. Even though he lived in a palace, he did not become attached to the riches around him. He lived much like a lotus flower on a lake, staying in contact with the water, yet remaining separate from it at all times.

From a very early age he developed another special ability. He could slip into deep and blissful meditation with great ease. He was able to fully focus his attention towards his soul, his inner being. So, he could easily avoid any distractions from the outside world.

6.

As a boy, Vardhaman was loved by everyone in the kingdom. He was a shining example of a prince, being handsome and healthy, but also courageous, strong and fearless.

One day, Vardhaman was playing in the palace garden with other young princes and he began to climb a tree. A fierce snake appeared and coiled itself around the trunk, hissing and spitting venom. Unknown to Vardhaman the snake was actually a fiendish heavenly being; which had transformed himself into a terrifying giant snake to test the Prince's bravery.

Vardhaman's playmates began to tremble with fear and run away. But Vardhaman was not frightened and without hesitation moved closer to the snake. Seeing his fearlessness, the angry snake became calm and changed himself back into a heavenly being. He then bowed to Vardhaman and called him Mahavir. The name means "great hero".

8.

Prince Vardhaman was visiting a city one day when he was confronted by a stampeding elephant. It was charging through the streets, causing chaos. People were screaming in fear as they tried to run away from the beast, which deafened them with his thunderous roars.

On seeing the crazed elephant, Vardhaman didn't try to escape but stood his ground in front of the huge animal. Confidently, he raised the palm of his right hand, in an effort to calm the elephant. The elephant quietened down and came to a steady halt.

Those who witnessed Vardhaman's bravery were amazed at what they had seen. He truly was a fearless prince.

10.

Not only was Vardhaman brave, he was also very intelligent. One day his friends came to the palace and asked King Siddhartha where they could find Vardhaman. The King, who was on the first floor, told them to look upstairs, so the boys ran to the top floor. Here they found Queen Trishla, who told them Vardhaman was downstairs.

The boys were very confused. How could Vardhaman be both upstairs and downstairs? They searched every floor and discovered Vardhaman on the middle floor, where he was studying. When they found him, the boys wondered who had been telling the truth, the King or the Queen. One had said Vardhaman was upstairs, and the other had said he was downstairs – surely they couldn't both be right?

Vardhaman told them that both his parents were correct. From where his father was on the first floor, he was upstairs, but from where his mother was on the top floor, he was downstairs. Many things in the world can be seen from different points of view, he explained to them. It just depends how you look at them.

When he reached the age of thirty, Vardhaman decided that he no longer wished to live the life of a royal prince. There were plenty of things in the palace to keep him busy and entertained. He realised that belongings didn't bring him joy. True happiness could only come from within.

He decided to become a Jain monk and live alone in the forest, focusing on the source of true happiness. He discarded his grand clothes and jewellery and plucked out all his hair with just his bare hands. His inner focus was so strong that this did not cause him any pain or distress. Heavenly beings came down to witness this momentous occasion, Vardhaman's transition from a prince to a monk.

14.

Monk Vardhaman would remain silent, never speaking to anybody. He was always engrossed in prayer and deep meditation.

When the dangerous animals of the forest saw his calm nature, and his simple, peaceful life, they forgot their predatory instincts. They became at ease with each other, and mongooses, snakes, tigers and cows would all drink water together from the same river. Wherever Monk Vardhaman went, the atmosphere was full of peace and tranquillity.

When he felt hungry, Monk Vardhaman would go to the nearest town. If a householder offered him pure food made according to the rules of Jainism, he would eat it and then return to the forest.

16.

Vardhaman spent twelve years as a monk, focusing on his inner self. The power of his focus grew stronger and stronger until he eventually attained a state of total happiness. He also developed complete knowledge of everything in the universe, past, present and future. The happiness and knowledge that he gained, would stay with him forever. He had now become Lord Mahavir, the twenty-forth Tirthankar; the god that he was destined to be. The visions in his mother's dreams had finally come true.

Heavenly beings created a glorious towering structure called a Samavasaran for Mahavir to sit on the top of and preach. He would make the sound "Om", which would vibrate across the land, to spread his wisdom far and wide. Humans, animals and heavenly beings would come in harmony to worship Mahavir as equals. They would attentively listen to his divine words, which they would understand in their own languages.

The day on which he first preached as a Tirthankar is celebrated in the whole of India as Veer Shasan Jayanti.

18

Tirthankar Mahavir spread his messages of peace, equality of all beings, and the path to true happiness across India for thirty years.

At the age of seventy-two years, on the day of Diwali, Mahavir left his body and attained nirvana, complete freedom. As a pure soul, he travelled to the very top of the universe to live in complete and everlasting happiness for eternity.

On the same day that Mahavir attained nirvana, his main follower, Indrabhuti Gautam, also became a god, in the same way as Mahavir. According to Jain tradition, the great festival of Diwali is celebrated in honour of Mahavir.

20.

Dedication to Veer

This book is written in dedication to my son Veer. He was named after Mahavir. Just like Mahavir, he too lives up to the meaning of his name – brave. It just so happens his birthday is also around that of Mahavir's birthday.

At the age of three we came to learn that Veer has a rare genetic disorder called Fanconi Anaemia. It means his bone marrow is not functioning properly, and so his blood counts are dropping. To fix this, he will need a stem cell transplant, for which we are searching for a matching stem cell donor.

To help Veer, and many others like him, to find the match they need, we are appealing to Asians to come forward and register as stem cell donors. We hope for a world where the donor pool is large enough, that anyone who needs a transplant in the future, has their match ready and waiting from day one. We don't want others to have to campaign like us. One day it could be someone you know who faces the same ordeal. By acting now, we can collectively fix this problem. It's in our hands.

Nirav Gudhka
Co-Author

To find out more about little Veer, and how to register as a stem cell donor, please visit www.helpveernow.org. You can also follow us on social media @HelpVeerNow.